JUL   2008

DISCARD

COLLECTION MANAGEMENT

1/14	9—	9/13

Special thanks to our adviser:
Susan Kesselring, M.A., Literacy Educator
Rosemount—Apple Valley—Eagan (Minnesota) School District

Cows Sweat Through Their Noses

and Other Freaky Facts About Animal Habits, Characteristics, and Homes

by Barbara Seuling

illustrated by Matthew Skeens

PICTURE WINDOW BOOKS

Minneapolis, Minnesota

Editor: Christianne Jones
Designer: Abbey Fitzgerald
Page Production: Michelle Biedscheid
Art Director: Nathan Gassman
The illustrations in this book were created digitally.

Picture Window Books
5115 Excelsior Boulevard
Suite 232
Minneapolis, MN 55416
877-845-8392
www.picturewindowbooks.com

Printed in the United States of America.

 All books published by Picture Window Books are manufactured with paper containing at least 10 percent post-consumer waste.

Library of Congress Cataloging-in-Publication Data
Seuling, Barbara.
Cows sweat through their noses: and other freaky facts about animal habits, characteristics, and homes / by Barbara Seuling; illustrated by Matthew Skeens.
p. cm. — (Freaky facts)
Includes index.
ISBN-13: 978-1-4048-3749-2 (library binding)
ISBN-10: 1-4048-3749-3 (library binding)
1. Animals—Miscellanea—Juvenile literature. I. Skeens, Matthew. II. Title.
QL49.S418 2008
590—dc22
2007004028

Table of Contents

Chapter 1

Tooth and Nail:
Physical Characteristics

Cows sweat through their noses.

Dogs sweat through their footpads.

Dalmatians are born without spots.

The Falabella pony of Argentina is quite small. It grows to be about the size of a large shepherd dog.

The giraffe has seven neck bones. That's the same number of neck bones as a mouse.

Giraffes are the only animals born with horns.

For many years it was believed that giraffes didn't make any sound at all. However, giraffes can make sound. But they usually use body language to communicate with other giraffes instead.

In one year, a single beaver can chew down hundreds of trees.

Beavers' teeth never stop growing. They wear away from chewing wood.

The yak's milk is pink.

Moose are so nearsighted that some have mistaken cars for their mates.

The shark doesn't have a bone in its body. Its skeleton is made of cartilage.

The shark's skin is covered with tiny teeth. The small teeth can scrape the skin off a human just by brushing against it.

A sharks teeth are lost and replaced throughout its entire life. It may have more than 30,000 teeth throughout its lifetime.

The lips of a hippopotamus are more than 24 inches (61 centimeters) wide.

Hippos' sweat is often red. The color comes from an oily substance that keeps a hippo's skin from drying and cracking.

Elephants have very good hearing. They can hear the footsteps of a mouse.

Elephants can't jump. They have the same bones in their feet as other animals, but their bones are more closely packed together. Because of this, they don't have the flexibility or spring that helps other animals jump.

The elephant's tusks are actually teeth. If the root of a tusk is infected, the pain can be so great that the elephant will pull it out by wedging it into a tree.

Like trees, frog bones grow new rings as they age.

In some places, giant land tortoise shells have been used as bathtubs.

The dugong is a large, gentle marine mammal. It has no tear ducts but appears to shed tears.

The sperm whale has the largest brain of any mammal.

A newborn blue whale can be longer than an adult elephant.

The octopus once had a shell. Its tentacles grew as its shell got smaller. Eventually the shell disappeared.

Sea stars don't have brains.

The sponge is an amazing sea creature. If it is squeezed through very fine mesh and divided into thousands of separate bits, the cells will rejoin to form another sponge.

The jellyfish is 99 percent water.

Cows give more milk when they listen to music. Some cows show a distinct liking for Mozart.

A blind chameleon can camouflage itself to match its surroundings.

A species of salamander called the cave newt is born with tiny eyes that eventually disappear. It doesn't need sight because its whole life is spent in dark underground caves.

The tuatara lizard of New Zealand is the only living creature to have three functional eyes—two in the usual place, and one on the top of its head.

The wings of bats are actually membranes of skin connecting long, slender fingers.

Birds can sing more than one song. The robin and the meadowlark have about 50 different songs.

Some bird couples sing duets, each bird singing different notes.

Night herons and barn owls glow in the dark.

The barn owl's face is shaped like a satellite dish. The shape helps it collect sound.

Woodpeckers don't get headaches when they hammer on hard wood. Their skull bones contain many air spaces, which act as shock absorbers.

The kiwi bird of New Zealand has tiny wings and cannot fly.

The kiwi bird has something no other bird has— nostrils at the tip of its beak. These help it smell worms underground.

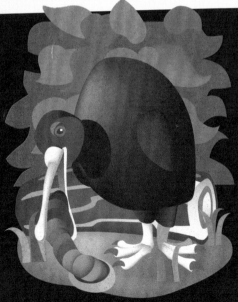

A pigeon's feathers are heavier than its bones.

The flamingo's ankles look like a human's knees.

Ants have five different noses.

Caterpillars have mouths, but butterflies don't.

Spiders have clear blood.

Every part of a newt can regenerate, even the jaws and eyes.

Snakes are deaf but can still tell when a human is approaching.

Six hundred and fifty houseflies weigh less than a paperclip.

Weaver
Plaza

Home Sweet Home:
Animal Shelters

Weaver birds build huge communal homes like apartment buildings. The homes can contain nearly 100 separate nests.

During the day, the oilbird lives deep inside mountain caves where it is totally dark. At dusk, the oilbird flies out only to search for food, then returns to the cave.

The bald eagle builds and then adds to its nest. One nest in Florida was 9.5 feet (2.9 m) wide and 20 feet (6.1 m) deep.

A few weeks after they are born, barnacles glue themselves to a surface and stay there for life. The substance they use to bond themselves to their home is stronger than any glue manufactured by people.

The peregrine falcon, which usually nests on high cliffs and canyons, has been known to nest on the windowsills of skyscrapers in New York City.

Kirtland's warbler, an endangered North American bird, depends on forest fires for its survival. Only the intense heat of a fire can burst open the tight cones of the jack pine tree, dispersing its seeds. These seeds eventually grow into a new forest of young pines, where the birds thrive. When the trees grow too tall, the birds leave and start over.

Millions of bats live inside the Carlsbad Caverns in New Mexico. Bats have been living in the caverns for 5,000 years.

Badgers air out their bedding in the spring.

The largest known beaver dam was built in Berlin, New Hampshire. It was 4,000 feet (1,220 m) long, which is the length of about 13 football fields.

The Mexican prairie dog's burrow is a hole that goes straight down. The animal must dive head first to enter.

Chapter Two

There can be more than 20,000 bees living in one hive.

Beehives are air-conditioned. In hot weather, bees place drops of water or diluted honey around the hive and fan their wings, keeping the hive cool.

Mole rats live in underground colonies in the same way that some insects do. Their underground colony is headed by a queen.

Sponges serve as houses for very small sea animals and plants. The sponge's passageways provide many compartments in which the tiny creatures can make their homes.

The Ross seal lives only on the floating ice of the Ross Sea in the Antarctic.

Hermit crabs don't have shells to protect their soft and vulnerable bodies. They usually use the cast-off shells of other creatures so they are protected from their enemies.

Some crabs will use anything they can find for a shell, including coconut shells, parts of lamps, plaster models, and soup cans.

Tasty Tidbits:
Eating Habits

The anglerfish has a kind of fishing rod growing out of its head. The rod has a lure at the end to attract other fish.

The leatherback turtle eats jellyfish. Unfortunately, the huge turtles sometimes swallow plastic bags, which look like jellyfish. The bags cause serious internal problems.

Galapagos tortoises eat anything that is red. Zookeepers often put their medicine inside tomatoes.

Baby sperm whales gain 200 pounds (90 kg) a day.

Baby blue whales drink more than 1 ton (0.9 metric ton) of milk a day.

Alligators weed their waterholes constantly. This keeps them free of tangled seaweed and water lily stems. This way, the alligators favorite food, turtles, will have a clear place to swim.

The pouch under a pelican's bill can hold almost 3 gallons (11 L) of water.

A shark can detect a fish's heartbeat before attacking and eating it.

There are land crabs that climb coconut trees to get food.

The tiny shrew has such a delicate nervous system and high metabolism that it can starve to death two or three hours after a meal.

Ants have found many clever ways to secure a food supply. Some keep gardens where they collect bits of leaves to use as compost for the raising of fungi. Others attack the seed and grain warehouses of other ant colonies and steal their food.

There's a kind of ant that bakes its own bread. It chews up grain, makes it into patties, and bakes it in the sun.

Honey ants become living storage tanks to hold food for the whole colony's use in emergencies. They eat until they grow into such huge balls that they can hardly move. During hard times, they spit up the stored food and share it with others.

For every one human in the world, there are 1 million ants.

A snake has no way to chew or bite off a piece of food. It has to swallow its food whole. For a snake to eat a large animal, the snake unhinges its lower jaws from either side of its skull.

Two-headed snakes are sometimes born. The two heads fight over food, even though it will go into the one stomach they share. When they are really angry, they might try to swallow each other.

Chapter Three

After chasing and killing prey, the cheetah needs half an hour to catch its breath before it can eat.

A lion needs to eat 11 to 15 pounds (5 to 7 kg) of meat every day. That's enough meat to feed 25 people.

The panda's diet is almost all bamboo. It eats about 88 pounds (40 kg) of bamboo a day.

Leopards drag their prey up into a tree to eat it

Wolves and wild dogs are able to swallow food and not digest it. When they arrive home after their hunt, they spit up the partially digested food to feed their young and those who stayed at home to guard the den.

Coyotes in Los Angeles have been known to sneak into the backyards of homes at night and drink water from the swimming pools.

In one day, a full-grown elephant can consume hundreds of pounds of food.

An adult elephant can drink up to 50 gallons (190 L) of water in one day.

When earthworms are plentiful, moles bite their heads off and store them underground. If moles forget where they put the worms, the worms can grow new heads and get away.

Baby robins eat 14 feet (4.3 m) of earthworms every day.

A heron wading in the water will hold a small feather in its beak and wait quietly for a fish to swim by. When it spots one, it drops the feather to attract the fish. As the fish goes toward the lure, the heron snatches its meal.

To crack open an ostrich egg, the Egyptian vulture drops stones on it.

The American giant water bug paralyzes its victim. Then it sucks all of the juices out of it.

Moving Right Along:
Getting Around

Tiny snails embed themselves in the mud on the feet of wading birds. When the birds move, the snails get a free ride.

Spiny lobsters march in single file lines when they migrate, each lobster holding on to the one in front of it.

Most sharks must keep moving, or they will sink. Most other fish have air bladders that make them weightless in water. But sharks are heavier than water, so they have to keep moving to stay up.

Cats have whiskers on the back of their front legs, as well as around their mouths. Their leg whiskers pick up air vibrations and help them get around in the dark.

Most rabbits are helpless in water, but one species, the marsh rabbit of the southeastern United States, swims and dives. When it wants to rest, it builds a raft of reeds, climbs aboard, and sails along.

A grizzly bear can run as fast as a horse.

Camels' feet are excellent for walking on sand. Each foot is made up of two big toes that are covered with thick, tough pads connected by a web of skin. In mud, however, the camel slips and slides and is nearly helpless.

Bees visit about 5 million flowers to make one average-size jar of honey.

The springtail, a type of insect, hops on a pogo-stick-like appendage. It can leap hundreds of times the height of its body.

Before monarch butterflies migrate, they sunbathe to gather enough heat to warm up their thoracic muscles, which control their wings.

Creeping slowly from one branch to another, the sloth rarely comes down out of the trees. If it does land on the ground, it has to walk on the sides of its feet because its toes are permanently curved into a hooked position. These hooks enable the animal to hang upside down. While hanging upside down, it eats, sleeps, mates, and even gives birth.

To get across a river, an armadillo gulps air until its stomach is full. Then it slides into the water and floats across like a balloon.

Some shrews are so small that they travel through tunnels dug by earthworms.

The only way a bat can get started in flight is to drop from its sleeping perch into the air. Once it is flying it cannot stop until it is ready to latch onto another perch.

Swans, ducks, and some other birds cannot fly during periods in which they are molting.

The ostrich can run as fast as a racehorse.

Penguins can't fly. But when they are underwater, they swim as though they were in flight. Their flippers and feet propel them swiftly through the water.

African jaçanas, birds also known as lily-trotters, walk across lily pads on their long toes without sinking into the water.

Mudskippers are fish that live in mangrove swamps along the Pacific Ocean and the Indian Ocean. When the tide is out, they use their fins as legs and can walk across the land until they come to more water.

The Abyssinian blue goose can fly backward.

The huge albatross, one of the world's largest flying creatures, is dependent on the wind for flight. Without a breeze, it cannot move and is trapped until a wind strong enough to move it comes along.

Hummingbirds can fly upside down, sideways, and backward, but they can't walk.

Hummingbirds hitch rides north tucked in the feathers of migrating Canada geese.

Flying squids travel in large schools. They often leap 18 feet (5.5 m) in the air, sometimes landing on the decks of passing ships.

Good Night, Sleep Tight:
Sleeping Habits

A curled-up, hibernating dormouse can be rolled across a table or tossed in the air and it won't wake up.

Many animals hibernate, or sleep through the winter, but none sleeps as soundly as the bat. Some bats have been found coated with ice, yet awaken as good as new when the weather gets warm.

Although all animals rest sometimes, it is believed that some do not really sleep. Goats, for example, rest about eight hours a day, but they never close their eyes.

Horses, giraffes, and some other four-legged animals sleep standing up. Giraffes will sometimes lean against a tree.

Seals sleep for only about one and a half minutes at a time.

When sea otters go to sleep at night, they wrap themselves in long strands of kelp to keep from being separated from their companions. During the night, they may drift far out to sea, tied together in the seaweed.

Elephants usually sleep standing up. If they lie down, they have to rock themselves from side to side to get their big bodies upright again.

One difference between moths and butterflies is that most moths sleep in the day and are active at night. Most butterflies sleep at night and are active during the day.

Swifts sometimes take naps by gripping the wings of flying airplanes with their feet.

Birds don't fall off their perches when they sleep because their toes lock in place around the twig or branch.

The huge albatross can sleep while it flies.

The blue-crowned hanging parrot sleeps hanging upside down like a bat.

Many seabirds sleep very little. The sooty tern, which rarely lands on water, may fly for several years with only brief periods of sleep lasting a few seconds each.

Parrotfish, which live in undersea coral caves, pull a blanket of mucus, or slime, over themselves when they go to sleep. In the morning, when they awake, they break out and swim away.

Baby chicks dream inside their eggs.

Glossary

appendage—a limb or other part that sticks out of an animal or plant

camouflage—a pattern or color on an animal's skin that makes it blend in with the things around it

cartilage—the strong, bendable material that forms some body parts on humans and animals

colonies—groups whose members live and work together

communal—used in common by members of the same group or community

compost—mixture of decaying leaves, vegetables, and other items that make the soil better for gardening

diluted—to make thin or weaker by adding liquid

dispersing—breaking up and scattering in different directions

ducts—tubes, pipes, or channels that carry a liquid or air

embed—to place firmly in something

fungi—forms of life that include mushrooms, molds, and mildews

kelp—a large, brown seaweed

lure—bait used in fishing; to attract something

mammal—a warm-blooded animal who feeds its babies milk

membranes—a thin, flexible layer of skin

mesh—a net made of threads or wires

migrate—to regularly move from place to place to find food, shelter, or a mate

molting—shedding fur, feathers, or an outer layer of skin

newt—a little salamander with stubby little legs and a long tail

prey—an animal that is hunted and eaten for food

reeds—tall grass with long, narrow leaves and joined stems

regenerate—to make new

regurgitate—throwing up incompletely digested food to feed others

shrew—a small animal that looks like a mouse

sloth—a slow moving animal that lives in the forests of South America

species—a group of animals that have similar characteristics

tentacles—long, thin body parts of certain animals

thoracic muscles—muscles in the thorax, which is located between the neck and the abdomen

thrives—is successful

tusks—very long, pointed teeth that stick out when the mouth is closed

Index

To Learn More

At the Library

De Ford, Deborah. *I Wonder Why Skunks Are so Smelly: And Other Neat Facts About Mammals*. Racine, Wis.: Western Pub. Co., 1992.

Greenway, Shirley. *Dragon, Dolphins, and Dinosaurs: Wacky Facts About Animals*. Boston: Whispering Coyote Press, 1993.

Mattern, Joanne and Ryan Herndon. *Guinness World Records. Astonishing Animals*. New York: Scholastic, 2005.

Rowen, Beth. *Time for Kids Almanac 2007 with Fact Monster*. New York: Time, Inc., 2007.

On the Web

FactHound offers a safe, fun way to find Web sites related to this book. All of the sites on FactHound have been researched by our staff.

1. Visit *www.facthound.com*
2. Type in this special code: 1404837493
3. Click on the FETCH IT button.

Your trusty FactHound will fetch the best sites for you.

Look for all of the books in the Freaky Facts series:

Ancient Coins Were Shaped Like Hams and Other Freaky Facts About Coins, Bills, and Counterfeiting

Cows Sweat Through Their Noses and Other Freaky Facts About Animal Habits, Characteristics, and Homes

Earth Is Like a Giant Magnet and Other Freaky Facts About Planets, Oceans, and Volcanoes

Three Presidents Died on the Fourth of July and Other Freaky Facts About the First 25 Presidents

Your Skin Weighs More Than Your Brain and Other Freaky Facts About Your Skin, Skeleton, and Other Body Parts